3/92

D0046838

CRUSADE *for* KINDNESS

Henry Bergh and the ASPCA

Books by John J. Loeper

GOING TO SCHOOL IN 1776
GOING TO SCHOOL IN 1876
THE HOUSE ON SPRUCE STREET

CRUSADE *for* KINDNESS

Henry Bergh and the ASPCA

by
John J. Loeper

ATHENEUM   1991   NEW YORK

Library of Congress Cataloging-in-Publication Data

Loeper, John J.
Crusade for kindness: Henry Bergh and the ASPCA / by John J.
Loeper. —1st ed.   p.   cm.
Includes bibliographical references.
Summary: Presents the life and accomplishments of Henry Bergh,
founder of the American Society for the Prevention of Cruelty to
Animals.
ISBN 0–689–31560–0

1. Bergh, Henry, 1811–1888—Juvenile literature.   2. Animal
welfare—United States—Juvenile literature.   3. Social
reformers—United States—Biography—Juvenile literature.
4. American Society for the Prevention of Cruelty to
Animals—History—19th century—Juvenile literature.   [1. Bergh,
Henry, 1811–1888.   2. Reformers.   3. American Society for the
Prevention of Cruelty to Animals—History.
4. Animals—Treatment.]   I. Title.
HV4764.L64   1991   179′.3′092—dc20   [B]   [92]   90–27682

Copyright © 1991 by John J. Loeper
All rights reserved. No part of this book may be reproduced or
transmitted in any form or by any means, electronic or mechanical,
including photocopying, recording, or by any information storage
and retrieval system, without permission in writing from the
Publisher.

Atheneum
Macmillan Publishing Company
866 Third Avenue
New York, NY 10022

Collier Macmillan Canada, Inc.
1200 Eglinton Avenue East
Suite 200
Don Mills, Ontario M3C 3N1

First edition
Printed in the United States of America
1 2 3 4 5 6 7 8 9 10

921
Bergh

*To Fred
and all the other animals
in my life*

Contents

CRUSADE for KINDNESS

Henry Bergh and the ASPCA

The dapper young Henry Bergh with top hat and cane
in a photograph taken about 1860

To The Reader

Humans and animals have always lived together, but their relationship has been confusing. Animals were worshiped and sacrificed; hugged and hunted; pampered and slaughtered. They serve us by providing food, clothing, and transportation. They can be our servants and our companions, our friends and our foes. As a result, our treatment of animals has often been cruel and inconsiderate.

Over the centuries, people have had to struggle to secure certain rights. People fought and died for freedom and equality under the law. That struggle continues today.

At the same time, certain people recognized the plight of animals. They recognized cruelty as cruelty regardless of its victim. They saw their own hurt and frustration in the eyes of dumb animals. Yet there were those who insisted that animals had no feelings. Animals were, as one philosopher put it, "mechanical robots." These people said that animals lacked sensation and could feel no pain. As a result, otherwise gentle and compassionate people treated animals horribly. Since animals felt no pain, most people saw nothing wrong when animal cruelty was presented as entertainment. Bears fought each other and cats were set on fire to amuse an audience. At one stage in history, most royal festivities included some animal cruelty.

Advances in science helped to change people's attitudes. The discovery of the microscope in the seventeenth century opened up unknown worlds and shattered old beliefs. Medical advances demonstrated that humans and animals shared similar organs. Even their brains were alike! Perhaps animals did feel pain. Slowly but surely, people began to question their interaction with other creatures.

It would be unjust not to mention certain people who preached kindness to animals when others were indifferent. Several ancient philosophers taught kindness to animals. And there were those like Saint Francis of Assisi, who preached love for all creatures. In America, there were anticruelty laws passed in the Massachusetts Bay Colony as early as 1641. In England and Ireland, there were laws protecting livestock. But the first real attempt to offer some protection to animals came about in England in 1824. In that year, the Society for the Prevention of Cruelty to Animals was founded. In 1840, Queen Victoria granted the society royal patronage. Its purpose was to take measures to prevent cruelty and to seek punishment for those found guilty of cruel treatment. The idea spread, and soon France, Germany, Belgium, and the Netherlands formed similar societies. The man who brought the idea to the United States was Henry Bergh.

"All honor to Henry Bergh, among the benefactors of our time," as a speaker praised him to a Boston audience in 1872. "The firm and unselfish advocate for that part of creation which cannot ask kind treatment for itself; the man who spoke effectually for those poor dumb mouths that have so long pleaded silently for protection from injury at the hands of men. It was a brave thing to have stood so many years between the oppressor and his quivering victim and to have borne so long the ridicule of those who cannot understand why a horse should not be overloaded. It is a sacred mission to which this man has been called. Among the world's benefactors he has proved himself a noble master of a difficult situation."

This is the story of that man—the story of Henry Bergh.

· 1813 ·
The Beginning

Henry Bergh, founder of the American Society for the Prevention of Cruelty to Animals (ASPCA), was born in New York City in 1813. This was during the presidency of James Madison, one year before Francis Scott Key composed "The Star-Spangled Banner," and Henry Bergh's birthplace was not the busy city he would know later on. At the time of his birth, there were fewer than one hundred thousand people crowded together in wooden houses on the lower part of Manhattan Island. Surrounding them were farms and forest. Because of its island location, New York was a busy seaport. Shipyards lined the East River up to the Battery.

Henry Bergh's father, Christian Bergh, owned one of these yards. He was descended from a German family that had emigrated to

America in 1700. Although Christian had been born at Rhinebeck on the Hudson, the Bergh family in 1789 had moved north to Canada. It was there, in the shipyards of Nova Scotia, that Christian Bergh had learned his trade. He married Elizabeth Ivers, and the couple later had settled in New York City, where Christian designed and built sailing vessels. Within a short time, he had become a wealthy and respected businessman. He built a large wooden house near his shipyard for his family, and his business prospered.

Henry Bergh was the youngest of Christian Bergh's three children. He was born on August 29, 1813, in the family home at Scammel and Water streets. A sister, Jane, was already five years old and a brother, Edwin, was eleven.

Old New York held many charms for the Bergh children. They played within sight and sound of their father's shipyard and watched the great ships come and go. The city streets were a medley of excitement. Sailors from foreign ports filled the air with unfamiliar words, and peddlers shouted their wares. Stagecoaches arrived daily from Boston, Philadelphia, and the southern colonies. Even the nights were exciting. There might be a torchlight parade marking some special event. Music and laughter escaped from the taverns and inns. And there were nightly fireworks and band concerts at the city park at Fort Clinton.

During summer afternoons, Henry and other neighborhood children could visit a small zoo owned by Henry Brevoort. This pet-loving New Yorker kept deer, tigers, and bears in his backyard. There were lots of other animals in the city too. Some families kept dogs and cats. Pigs, goats, and cattle roamed the streets, and horses and mules pulled carriages, wagons, and streetcars.

Despite this, Henry gave little indication of his future passion for animal rights. He seemed interested only in pretty girls and having a good time. Women noticed him too. He had large blue eyes and a mass of dark curls. His practical German father must have worried about his younger son. Although Edwin graduated from Georgetown University with honors, Henry dropped out of school. Parties and dances, rather than study, held his attention. One of his teachers called him "rich and lazy"!

New York, being a Dutch settlement, celebrated each New Year's with great festivity. Most families had open houses. New Yorkers

Henry Bergh at the time of his marriage

could visit home after home, enjoying a variety
of food and drink. It was at one of those open-
house parties on New Year's Day in 1839 that
Henry Bergh met his future wife, Matilda Taylor. She was the daughter of a wealthy English-
man, and it was love at first sight! Later that
same year, they announced their engagement.
The wedding was to take place at Saint Mark's
Church in Manhattan. But on the morning of
the wedding, Henry and Matilda threw caution

to the wind and eloped. Much to the consternation of their families and the surprise of their guests, they never arrived at the church.

Shortly after Henry's elopement, Christian Bergh died. Three years later, Christian's wife died. Though the three Bergh children had lost their parents, they had inherited a considerable fortune. Some estimates placed it over one million dollars. The shipyard closed down, and the family house was sold. With little to hold them in New York, Henry and Matilda decided to travel in Europe. They went in style and stayed at the best hotels. Henry learned a bit of French and Italian, while Matilda shopped for jewelry and clothing. They were a rich and fashionable young couple and made many new friends. They were invited to balls and dinner parties and thoroughly enjoyed their travels.

During their stay in Europe, there were some hints of Henry's future course. In Spain, he took note of a cart driver whose voice "filled his horse with terror." In Greece, he wrote, "The horses are worse off than in Spain. Whenever the horses do not go as fast as the driver desires, he strikes the animals in the face with his fist." But it was at a bullfight in Seville where Henry's sensibilities were offended. "About twenty-five horses and eight bulls were destroyed today," he wrote. He was so upset by what he saw that he wrote a letter to a New York newspaper. In it, he protested the slaughter of the bullring. His letter appeared in print in June of 1848.

At home again in America, Henry and Matilda Bergh continued to enjoy their wealth and social position. Henry built a large house on Fifth Avenue and lived the life of a prosperous man. He had influential friends and knew the important people of his day. One of his New York neighbors was the governor of the state.

For a while, Henry tried his hand at writing. He fancied himself a poet and playwright. A few of his efforts did succeed in reaching print, but then one critic wrote, "There is positively no merit in them."

· 1863 ·
A Diplomatic Assignment

The Berghs spent the winter of 1858 at the fashionable Willard Hotel in Washington. Despite the gathering storm clouds of the Civil War, the nation's capital was filled with fun and parties. Henry and Matilda became part of the Washington scene and attended many social gatherings. They mingled with important people and politicians. One of these was William Henry Seward, later to become secretary of state to President Abraham Lincoln.

Later that same year, the Berghs departed for another stay in Europe. This time they remained there almost three years. During this stay, Henry was presented at court to Queen Victoria and Prince Albert. He and Matilda also visited Russia, staying for a while in the capital city of Saint Petersburg (presently Leningrad).

The Berghs liked Russia. They were impressed by the glitter of Russia's royalty and the people's attitude toward Americans. "There are many points of resemblance between Russia and the United States," Henry wrote to a friend.

Eventually, the Berghs returned home to America, but they did not stay there for long. Early in 1863, President Lincoln appointed Henry to the post of legation secretary at the court of Czar Alexander II in Saint Petersburg. He would serve under the American ambassador, Cassius Clay.

On July 12, 1863, the Berghs returned to Russia. A month after arriving in Saint Petersburg, Henry wrote, "I am thoroughly at work in my official position and like it amazingly."

The Russia of 1863 was a land of stark contrasts. Saint Petersburg was a sophisticated and beautiful city. Peter the Great had spared no effort in making his new capital a place of comfort and beauty. Yet, much of the rest of the country lived in primitive conditions. The czar resided in luxurious palaces, like the Winter Palace in Saint Petersburg, surrounded by noble families. These privileged few controlled the wealth of Russia. Four-fifths of the population, or forty-eight million people, were serfs or peasants, half owned by noble families and the other half by the czar. Serfs were desperately poor and victims of disease. They were illiterate and malnourished. Expected to give all of their energy and even their lives to Mother Russia, they received little in return.

Czar Alexander II did try to free the serfs and give them certain rights, but their complete emancipation would take a long, long time. For example, they still remained subject to corporal punishment. It was not unusual to see a peasant beaten or whipped for some minor offense, and a serf's life was always in danger.

In such an atmosphere, cruelty to animals was commonplace. If most humans had few rights, animals had none. Often, the peasants took out their frustrations on their animals. A lazy horse was beaten, a stray dog was stoned, or a howling cat was scalded. Cruelty was part of life.

Henry saw this mistreatment of animals. On one occasion, he scolded a driver who was whipping a horse. The more cruelty he saw, the angrier he became. "Mankind is served by animals," he said, "and in turn they receive no protection."

Henry Bergh's sudden passion over animal abuse puzzled his friends. He had witnessed cruelty elsewhere, but it was his stay in Russia that changed his life. "At last I have found a way to be of use," he told them. For whatever the reason, animals had a new and powerful friend.

· 1865 ·
The Birth of a Movement

On their return from Russia in 1865, Henry and Matilda stopped over in England. Henry found that the idea of kindness to animals had already found acceptance there. He went to London to meet with Lord Harrowby, president of England's Royal Society for the Prevention of Cruelty to Animals. The society was then in its forty-first year. It worked to enact legislation protecting animals and it supported animal rescue. After weeks of discussions with Lord Harrowby, Henry decided to form a similar society in the United States. Merciful treatment of animals, he told Lord Harrowby, was "the long cherished dream of my heart."

Henry Bergh was the first to admit that he had never been especially interested in animals. He was not devoted to pets, and his concern for animals was not sentimental. Rather, he recognized the injustice of it all. He would speak for those creatures unable to speak for themselves.

Returning to New York, Henry made his plans and prepared for his crusade. On a stormy night in early February of 1866, he spoke before a small but select audience at New York's Clinton Hall. Included among the invited guests was a future mayor of New York City and several millionaire businessmen. Henry presented his case.

"Last evening," reported the *New York Times* on February 9, "Henry Bergh delivered a lecture on 'Statistics Relating to the Cruelties Practiced upon Animals' . . . with a view to the establishment of a society kindred to that so long in successful operation in London and other cities of Great Britain and Ireland."

In his speech, Henry denounced the brutalities of vivisection, or experimenting on live animals. He talked about the abuse of the horses used to pull the streetcars in the city, and he denounced the cruel things done in slaughterhouses.

"This is a matter of conscience," he told his audience. "It is a moral question in all its aspects. It is a solemn recognition of that greatest attribute of the Almighty—mercy."

No one in New York City or elsewhere in the United States had to look hard to find cruelty to animals. Some of the things happening were much worse than the horse beatings of Russia. The country had just fought a civil war over the issue of human rights. It had not tackled the issue of animal rights. Its cities were badly overcrowded with people and with animals. Pigs and chickens roamed city streets, and horses were used to pull every load. Dogs and cats were everywhere, some with homes, most without. Everywhere animals suffered and had no one to speak for them.

Henry asked his influential friends and acquaintances to sign a document entitled "A Declaration of the Rights of Animals." Among the signatures were those of the mayor of New York, a future governor, two Roosevelts, the millionaire John Jacob Astor, the Harper brothers of publishing fame, and many other men of wealth and power. Next, Henry journeyed to Albany to ask the New York legislature for a charter incorporating his ASPCA. Despite some opposition, the society was chartered on April 10, 1866.

The next task was to obtain passage of a law

ALBUQUERQUE ACADEMY
LIBRARY

An 1865 magazine illustration shows men clubbing a horse
in an attempt to make the animal work harder.
It was later adapted for the seal of the ASPCA.

protecting animals. Although New York had
such legislation, it was weak and rarely en-
forced. Henry wanted a law passed that provided "that every person who shall, by his act or
neglect, maliciously kill, maim, wound, injure,
torture or cruelly beat any horse, mule, cow,
cattle, sheep or other animal belonging to himself or another, shall, upon conviction, be ad-
judged guilty of a misdemeanor." Punishment
for a misdemeanor was imprisonment for not
more than one year, or a fine, or both.

The law was passed because of the many powerful friends Henry had on his side. Henry's society had some muscle. With the establishment of The ASPCA and the passage of strong legislation, Henry Bergh began the first organized struggle against cruelty to animals in America. There were others, of course, who had spoken out before him. Some states did have animal legislation, although it was very weak and most often tied to property rights. And, before the Revolution, Thomas Paine, the voice of the colonial cause, wrote, "Everything of cruelty to animals is a violation of moral duty. We serve God by contributing to the happiness of the living creation which God has made." But now there would be action!

Henry Bergh became the chief officer and the voice of his American Society for the Prevention of Cruelty to Animals (ASPCA). He had found a purpose and meaning in life. He was no longer the writer or diplomat or world traveler; now his life belonged to animals. The beaten horse, the mistreated calf and pig, the tortured cat, and the thousands of stray dogs on the city streets had a friend.

He established headquarters for the society in two small rooms at Broadway and Fourth

Street. They were dingy quarters, and poorly furnished. Henry intended to use any money the Society had raised to promote animal welfare. One day a visitor stumbled over a hole in the carpet. "Mr. Bergh," he insisted, "please buy a new carpet and send the bill to me."

"No, thank you," Henry replied, "but please send the money, and I will put it to better use for my animals."

·1866·
The Crusade Begins

Henry Bergh began patrolling the streets of Manhattan in search of animal abuse. He always wore a top hat and carried a cane. And he wore a badge, the symbol of his legal authority.

At first, Henry gave polite warnings to offenders. He soon discovered that these meant little. He decided to get tough and he enlisted the help of the city police. He intended to arrest those breaking the new statute against animal cruelty. His initial arrest was a Brooklyn butcher. The man was observed driving a cart filled with calves, their legs tightly bound with rope. The head of one calf jolted against a sharp piece of wood every time the wagon bounced along. It threatened to gouge out the animal's eye. The butcher was brought to court and fined. It was the first conviction won by the ASPCA. Others followed. The next day there were three more arrests. In each case, the offender was fined, and one even served a day in prison. The days following brought new arrests.

After a month passed, Henry called a meeting of the society to report on his accomplishments. At the same time, bylaws for the organization were adopted, and annual dues were set at ten dollars. Andrew Johnson, then president of the United States, was made an honorary member of the society.

As time went by, more people offered their help. Some donated money; others gave their time and effort. Among the first to help Henry in patrolling the streets was a young black man. Another was a schoolboy. They reported instances of animal abuse to the ASPCA.

But, despite the help and sympathy of a few, the greatest problem was public apathy. Most people were blind to animal abuse or just did not care to hear about it. The humane treatment of animals was a very new idea!

In the spring of 1866, Henry investigated a complaint that chickens were being plunged into boiling water and plucked while alive. He investigated and made an arrest. When the case came to court, the defense argued that chickens did not fall under the law. The law, the lawyer argued, was meant for "noble creatures," not for lowly chickens.

In the late 1800s, there was a coarseness in city life. In a nation that had just rid itself of human slavery, animal abuse was a minor issue. Pigeon shoots were held in which live birds were first blinded in one eye or had a wing broken. This created a more varied flight pattern and added a challenge to the shoot. Ordinary people flocked to dogfights, where dogs either fought each other or fought rats. At one, Sportsman Hall, dogs were forced to fight black bears. On the streets, sick and lame horses strained to pull streetcars. More often than not, these cars were jammed with riders. It was not unusual to see parts of the leather harness embedded in a horse's flesh. The wretched condition of these streetcar horses was well-known. In the city dog pounds, dogs and cats were cruelly slaughtered or clubbed to death.

These were the things Henry had to face. He was everywhere, fearlessly raiding the dog fights or rescuing injured and sick animals. He also wrote newspaper articles promoting the work of the ASPCA.

Eventually, one special case brought Henry

and the ASPCA the publicity they needed to arouse the public. The opportunity was the arrival of the schooner *Active* with a load of South American turtles bound for the Fulton Fish Market. Acting on a tip, Henry investigated conditions aboard the ship. Henry found hundreds of large turtles on their backs, half-dead of thirst and starvation. Holes had been bored through their fins so that ropes could be drawn through them to hold them down.

The captain and his crew were arrested. At court, the defense attorneys declared that the turtle was not an animal; therefore, no law was broken. What then was it? Henry countered. Was it a mineral or a vegetable? Although he lost the case, the newspaper coverage gave him the publicity he needed to promote his work. One city paper devoted six columns to the turtles. Other papers ridiculed Henry and the ASPCA. But the important result was that people everywhere were talking. At least they knew now that there was an organization fighting for the rights of all animals.

Shortly after the turtle incident, a city restaurant featured a live turtle resting on a pillow in its dining room. Above it was this sign:

Having no desire to wound the feelings of the SPCA or of its president, Henry Bergh, we have done what we could for the comfort of this poor turtle during the few remaining days of its life. He is appointed unto death, however, and will be served in soups and steaks on Thursday. Come dine and do justice to his memory.

Certain newspapers were especially critical. They accused Henry of using the ASPCA for his personal gain. One wrote:

The mild and gentle looks of the poor calves and doomed chickens touches the heart of the gentle Bergh. All will be set right as soon as the new millennium is realized and Negro-sufferage and the rights of pigs and poultry to life, liberty and the pursuit of happiness is established. The officers of the SPCA live like parasites on the public. They belong to the same party whose humanitarian tenderness stirred up a Civil War.

Despite the attacks, Henry continued his crusade. "I fear neither disease nor ridicule," he wrote. "From early morning until ten o'clock at night, I am at work. My own private affairs are neglected and I am often scolded by Mrs. Bergh for not giving a little time to personal matters." But often, when the ridicule and abuse became too severe, Henry would burst into tears in the privacy of his home.

The society became his reason for living. He not only gave it his time, but he also endowed it with much of his property. How the change in him must have puzzled his friends. His entire life was now devoted to the cause of animals. Henry Bergh was the life and heart of the ASPCA.

As time passed, the movement grew. Branches were established in surrounding boroughs. In Brooklyn, there was a separate SPCA. In 1867, Buffalo organized an SPCA. Pennsylvania chartered one in 1868. Another began in Boston and another in San Francisco. By 1869, Maine, New Jersey, and Canada had started societies. All of these SPCAs—with hundreds yet to come—functioned independently. Henry Bergh's group was the American Society for Prevention of Cruelty to Animals. Similar groups used Society for Prevention of Cruelty to Animals in their titles. Yet, all SPCAs owed allegiance and loyalty to Henry Bergh. He was the source of their inspiration and their role model. His idea had taken root and his crusade was spreading from coast to coast.

·1868·
The Poor Horses!

In the early nineteenth century, no creature came in for greater abuse than draft horses. These were the hardworking animals that pulled carts, wagons, coaches, and the city streetcars. These humble creatures often bore the human reactions to the frustrations of a horse-drawn age. New York, especially, was a city vexed with transportation problems. Its streets were overcrowded with a mad jumble of streetcars, private coaches, carts, and wagons. There was a perpetual traffic jam. In winter, thousands of sleighs replaced the carriages.

In 1832, New York had started the first horse-drawn street railway in the world. Hundreds of cars pulled by teams of horses bobbed along miles of track. These horsecars were as indispensable as today's subways and buses. They were always crowded with passengers and,

Two horses try to pull an overloaded streetcar
in New York City.

during rush hours, were packed with humanity. A popular verse of the day describes the
situation:

Never full, pack 'em in.
Move up, fat man! Squeeze in, thin!
Forty seated, forty standing,
Forty more on either landing.

The only concern expressed for the poor horses forced to haul this mass of people was on the grounds of human discomfort. "They should either build larger cars or get stronger horses," one newspaper commented.

No one, except Henry Bergh and the ASPCA, took notice of the poor horses. The injustice of making a pair of sickly nags strain to pull an overloaded car escaped most people's attention. It was even worse in wintertime when the animals slipped and skidded over icy streets, when salt used to melt the ice burned their feet. And how were the horses handled? They were whipped. In the 1860s, over twenty million horsewhips were manufactured annually. It was not unusual to see horses, their bloody backsides covered with snow, straining to pull streetcars through drifts.

Henry Bergh and his agents stopped overcrowded cars and arrested drivers. They made passengers disembark to lighten the load. On one occasion, Henry caused gridlock in the midtown streets. He stopped an overloaded car and would not allow it to move until it unloaded excess passengers. Henry held his ground even when people refused to leave the

Henry Bergh stops an overcrowded streetcar.

car. All the traffic around it was brought to a halt.

Obviously, the streetcar companies were not pleased. They constantly fought legislation that would limit the number of passengers a car could carry. But limitation laws were passed in New York and in other cities. The Pennsylvania SPCA reported, in 1869, that a guilty verdict had been obtained against the driver of an overloaded car in Philadelphia. A similar victory was hailed in Massachusetts.

In February of 1868, Henry Bergh wrote an

indignant letter to the president of the New York streetcar line. In it he described an incident.

Last night, almost exhausted with labors of the day, I saw on the Bowery one of your horses which had fallen from simple overwork. The poor animal was lame, and his body had sores upon it. Its driver said that it was very sick and had been for some time; but that your man in charge insisted on it being driven! The result was that nature gave out, and the poor, outraged beast, with a loud groan, fell upon the ice-bound street, and would have died had I not stopped and devoted an hour to its care. When too fatigued to do much more, I went home with a heavy heart, saddened more than I can express and, perhaps, to be laughed at for my pains.

The cruelties of the horsecar age called for all the zeal and courage Bergh and his society could muster. "Bergh makes himself ridiculous," one newspaper complained. "One is compelled to believe him insane or to conclude that he is a mere seeker after personal notoriety at the expense of public convenience."

Another cause for concern was the housing of the streetcar animals. The horsecar companies themselves admitted that some of their stables were "horse hells." They were filthy and badly ventilated. They were also firetraps. Fire department statistics showed that hundreds of horses were burned to death each year in stable fires. To make matters worse, many stables had several floors. Horses stored above the ground floor had no chance to escape a fire. In one, twelve hundred horses roasted to death.

Henry Bergh tried to attack the problem through legislation. He proposed to make ground-floor storage of animals mandatory. Most people thought he was silly. One cartoon entitled "It Even Makes The Animals Laugh," pictured Henry with a huge pair of donkey ears holding a petition and an escape ladder.

As time went by, electric trolley cars replaced the horsecars. Many of the abuses disappeared with the change. But Henry Bergh fought on. Carriage owners who allowed uncovered horses to stand in bitter cold weather were cited. The use of cruel whips and goads and reins was denounced. "Those fearful iron inventions," Henry called them. The most cruel

A magazine cartoon ridicules Bergh's suggestion to provide a fire escape for animals.

of the lot was the cheek rein. This was a leather pad covered with sharp needles. It was designed to puncture the cheeks of the horse, causing it to prance and rear. This gave the appearance of high spirits. "It makes the horse move magnificently," the owner insisted. "A magnificent agony," Henry countered.

Henry Bergh preached that all sensitive and responsible people owed a debt to the animals that served them. This was especially true of the horse. To be insensitive to the suffering inflicted on a workhorse, he warned, was immoral in a civilized society. It took many years and much effort before his message was understood.

This was evident in the ultimate fate of most workhorses. They were sold at horse markets. Here, old and sickly horses were bought for a few dollars to drag the wagons of icemen and hucksters until they dropped dead. Old horses were treated much like old cars today. They were the "junkers" of their day and provided cheap transportation. The oldest and most sickly were sold as "skinners": They were bought for their hides. ASPCA agents began to visit these markets and buy up the old horses. They were then either placed on farms owned by the society or put to a quick and humane death.

In 1869, Henry Bergh wrote the following letter to a horse owner.

This morning you gave a worn-out horse to a boy to be led to the Horse Market to be sold. This creature had probably given you his labor as long as he was able. When he could be of no further use, common humanity should cause you to put an end to his suffering, not send him to be tortured to death, as you well know what happens to horses sold at the Market.

The few dollars you might get for him may blister your hands and soul. When that most useful of all man's servants is unfit for further service, it is the duty of good men to mercifully kill them. Prosperity will never come to those who abuse the dumb and speechless of God's creation.

· 1869 ·
The Slaughterhouses and the Dairies

Henry Bergh was a gentle man. His nature and his background did not prepare him for the cruelties he would encounter and oppose. His crusade demanded a large measure of personal courage. Nowhere was this courage needed more than in his routine visits to the city slaughterhouses. He had to steel himself to face their terror and gore. The horror was beyond belief. In most instances, butchering was done without any regard for the animal. Pigs were skinned alive; calves were hung on hooks for hours before the butcher came along to kill them. The skull of an ox or sheep was pounded with an ax. Many of the butchers were without mercy. In dismay, he asked one butcher, "How can you sleep at night after such daily horror?"

It is not likely that any of the butchers lost sleep over their work. Most of them were tough and insensitive. They had to be. The animals had to be slaughtered, and it was their job to do it. They answered Bergh with ridicule and threats. In anger, they threw bloody entrails at him. They insulted and mocked him.

But Henry Bergh pressed on. "Remember," he told them, "the same starlit night that brings you rest shines down also upon the blood-stained stones of your slaughterhouses and upon the dumb, despairing sufferers there."

He tried to convince them that animals had feelings, that they suffered terror and felt pain. This was a novel idea. There were educated people who still believed that animals were insensitive to pain and suffering. Being concerned about their welfare was considered silly and a waste of time. Henry Bergh and his followers insisted that animals did feel pain and fright. They did not mean to eliminate butchering, but to ensure a swift and merciful death for the animals.

Despite the threats and abuse, Bergh continued to patrol the slaughterhouses and demand reform. Several of the large meat companies fought him. They tried to restrain the ASPCA from interfering in "the lawful exercise of business." They brought legal action, but

Sick and dying cattle wait to be slaughtered.

the courts upheld the efforts of the society. These victories helped to establish the rights of animals.

Henry Bergh was not a vegetarian. He accepted the killing of animals for food, but he demanded that they be given a kind and speedy death. Butchering was a necessary evil, but it did not have to be barbaric.

This was not a completely new idea. A century earlier, Benjamin Franklin suggested electrocution in place of slaughter as a kinder means of death. Several European countries had laws governing slaughter. One such law prevented animals from witnessing the slaughter of their companions. This helped reduce the animal's fear while awaiting its turn.

But in most American slaughterhouses, animals were routinely killed with clumsy cruelty. "Does a creature condemned to death in order to nourish and sustain human life lose all claim to mercy?" Henry asked. After one day spent investigating, Bergh wrote, "The sights I have seen today surpass anything that the imagination can depict! Cruelty to animals fails to express it. I am tired out and sick, and shall go home to bed. I could see no more and contain myself. But tomorrow my officers shall make arrests and put a stop to these hellish practices."

Eventually, people listened to Henry Bergh and his pleas for mercy. Humane treatment finally found its way into the slaughterhouse. Killing became swift, and needless suffering was eliminated. "There's Bergh!" a butcher shouted on one occasion. "We better behave ourselves!"

Another pressing problem was the transport of animals to market. Lambs were packed together in boxcars and often smothered to death. Cattle shipped from the western ranches went for days without food or water. They were prodded and jabbed with pitchforks. It was not unusual for one to have an eye poked out in the process. A Chicago newspaper reported:

> *The manner in which animals are crowded together in narrow cars, their unappeased thirst during days and nights of dusty riding, their hunger and fatigue, and, finally, the wanton cruelties to which butchers subject them before terminating their unhappy lives—all affect their flesh rendering it less nutritious. It is this which gives a practical character to societies for the prevention of cruelty to animals. We learn with sincere pleasure that an effort is being made in this city to start such a society.*

Sheep and calves are transported to the slaughterhouse.

This notion—that humane treatment and slaughter would improve the taste and quality of meat—helped Bergh's crusade. As the newspaper suggested, it made the entire matter "practical." Both the public and the meat companies became convinced that reforms were necessary. But the struggle for reform was long and hard. It was only because of the constant visits by animal rights activists to the slaughterhouses and the insistent demands for humane treatment that change came about. Animals were treated with consideration and were slaughtered quickly. Justice and pity won, and Henry became a symbol for the rights of animals.

Later on, the *New York Times* paid Bergh this tribute:

Humanitarian ideas prevail in the city. Rabbits and calves are butchered with but small pain. Anyone who remembers past practice will recognize the enormous improvement, for which the public is almost wholly indebted to Henry Bergh.

In helping animals, Henry Bergh often helped people to improve their own lot. His crusade benefited humans as well as animals. Reforms in the slaughterhouses imposed more sanitary conditions and made meat safer to eat. The same thing happened when Henry and the ASPCA moved against the city dairies.

Before the late nineteenth century, when the French biologist Louis Pasteur developed his process for the sterilization of milk, drinking milk could be unhealthy and dangerous. Pasteurization was unheard of, and dairies were rarely inspected. It was common practice to feed milk cows slop, or "swill." This was garbage from restaurants and slaughterhouses mixed with water. It was used as a cheap feed in place of hay. Cows were crowded into narrow stalls without ventilation. They were given no food other than the swill, and this poor diet made most of them ill. Unhealthy cows give unhealthy milk.

After one inspection of a stable in Brooklyn, Henry Bergh reported:

These foul prisons show man's stupidity and cruelty. Animals wallow in filth; some tied by the neck in their narrow stalls by rope or chain; others are fastened by each horn so as to forbid movement; and in the trough before

them is an acrid swill which no living crea-
ture would take into its stomach. In some
instances, animals are actually dying while
being milked. And this milk is sold as "Pure
Milk."

As with the slaughterhouses, Henry Bergh's attacks on the dairies were met with hostility and ridicule. "His society is a humbug!" one city official sneered. "He is more to be pitied than blamed. Men possessing but a single idea are sometimes given to outrageous and incorrect statements."

But Henry Bergh pressed on. In January of 1870, he prodded the New York Board of Health to join him and ASPCA officers in a tour of dairies. Several newspaper reporters joined the group. One situation was as bad as the next. Feeding troughs were slimed with swill, and the stench was unbearable. "It took heroism on the part of Mr. Bergh and his companions to continue the inspection," one reporter noted. Finally the Board of Health was shamed into action. Dairies and milk dealers were fined and became subject to regular inspections.

"I want people to become aware of what they eat and drink," Henry told others. "I find cows standing with great ulcers upon them. And yet, when I attempt to bring this state of things to light, there is a howl raised. Bergh exaggerates. Bergh sees things through colored glass. When I took the president of the Board of Health to visit cattle sheds, he was amazed, and said that he had not the least idea of the magnitude of the evil. Let those who charge me with exaggeration visit the cattle pens with me."

Eventually, sanitary laws put an end to the horrible situation Henry Bergh had exposed. As a result, people consumed safe and healthy milk and milk foods in place of the dangerous products of the past.

·1870·
Man's Best Friend

If horses and farm animals had to be rescued from cruelty, so did man's best friend, the dog.

At the time, some dogs were used as beasts of burden, to pull carts and to work treadmills. Treadmills were mill wheels turned by a dog walking on a continuous belt.

One of the first tasks of the ASPCA was gaining passage of a law requiring a license for a dog to draw a cart. This gave some control over the use of the animal. As with horses, it was not unusual for cart dogs to be overworked and overburdened.

Using dogs on treadmills was allowed by law as long as the dog was not cruelly treated, but inspections were not carried out routinely. Dogs were forced to walk until they dropped from exhaustion. Often their harnesses would

An 1866 newspaper illustration shows dogs
pulling a garbage cart.

cut into their flesh. These cruelties were exposed by the ASPCA.

An even greater problem than the treadmill
dogs or the cart dogs were the strays. A bounty
was paid on stray dogs. Dog "collectors"
roamed the city streets, capturing any dog they
could find. These were held at the city dog
pounds.

A terror on the city streets was the dog-
catcher. These political appointees were paid a
salary to hunt the streets for stray dogs, which
they then brought to the pound. They captured
puppies and dogs wherever they found them. At
the pounds, the animals were jammed into
crowded pens.

Each afternoon, unclaimed dogs were drowned. The pound master placed sixty to eighty dogs in a large vat, then bolted on a cover and filled the vat with water. One pound master devised a more efficient system. He filled an iron cage with dogs and lowered it into the East River. At other times, dogs were knocked on the head with a club, shot, drowned, and beaten.

In St. Louis, Missouri, it was reported that a

Stray dogs from the New York City dog pound are drowned in the river.

A cartoon pokes fun at Henry Bergh's concern
over the fate of stray dogs.

pound keeper clubbed dogs to death until "the
floor of the pen was slippery with blood." Another pound keeper hanged dogs. In a southern
city, strays were lassoed and beaten to death.

"Will no one speak for the dogs?" the magazine *Puck* asked. Next to the text was a cartoon
showing Henry Bergh as "The Only Mourner."

Over and over gain, Bergh protested the cruel
treatment of dogs in the city pounds. He constantly checked the activities of the dogcatch-
ers, and he worked to establish proper shelters
for stray dogs.

In 1871, Philadelphia claimed credit for being the first American city to replace its pound with a shelter. Here strays and mongrels had food and water and space to run. Condemned dogs were put to death humanely with gas. The Philadelphia shelter was the work of the Pennsylvania SPCA and it served as a model during Henry Bergh's lifetime.

One of the most terrible uses of dogs was in dogfighting. Dogfighting, ratting, cockfighting, and other blood sports were illegal in most states. Yet a day seldom passed in most American cities without an animal fight. It was considered a great sport, and the events drew large crowds.

Animals were placed in a pit at the center of an amphitheater. Some amphitheaters held as many as four hundred people. The pits were the scenes of bloody contests between dogs, or dogs set against bears or rats. Bets were taken, and the crowd called for blood. In one fight between two pit bulls, the loser's head was "a mass of blood, her jaws, jagged and torn, one ear torn away and not a kick left in her."

Henry Bergh and his ASPCA sought out these fights and raided them. They invoked the law

Men gather around to watch a dogfight.

prohibiting them and demanded that the promoters be prosecuted.

"Ratting [dogs and rats fighting] has been put down by the irrepressible suppressor of cruelty to animals, Mr. Bergh," one newspaper complained. "There used to be grand fights and rattings in the 'good old times,' but now they never occur. The pits are empty."

But another paper supported Henry Bergh's vigilance. It called the fights "a burlesque on civilization and a farce. To see one is to become disgusted."

"A sport should not be the enjoyment of cruelty and bloodshed. This shows our barbarism," Henry Bergh preached. "Let us have healthful and invigorating sport to take the place of these animal fights. Americans seek diversion and amusement but they are not willing to give over their country to bloody and demoralizing scenes. The civilization of a people is indicated by their treatment of animals."

· 1872 ·
The Movement Spreads

Stories about Henry Bergh and his work spread throughout the country. By 1872, eighteen states and territories had established associations to prevent cruelty to animals.

While his doctrine about the rights of all creatures spread, Bergh continued his work in New York. Most days and nights he patrolled the city streets, seeking out instances of animal abuse. He rescued dogs and cats and horses. He fought for the humane treatment of all living things. He urged that children be taught kindness. "Let the child learn," he said, "that there is no being so insignificant as to be unworthy of protection, be it a worm that crawls on the ground, or the suffering orphan or widow."

Bergh and his ideas continued to be ridiculed. Yet, despite criticism, his crusade was taking hold. Humane societies multiplied.

His courage was tested on many occasions. He received numerous anonymous letters bearing threats against his life. One named the day and hour of his assassination! Among his tormentors were several city newspapers. The *New York Sunday Mercury* called him "an Ass that should have his ears cropped." Another newspaper ridiculed, "Rats insist on having a chair at the table . . . goats put on airs . . . hogs grunt with delight . . . as unlimited sway is given to the very humane Bergh."

But nothing could stop him. His work went on. He put an ambulance wagon into service for sick and lame animals. He established shelters and rest farms for old animals. And he

A horse ambulance designed by Henry Bergh

A derrick designed by Henry Bergh for lifting fallen horses

went about the country giving lectures to promote his ideas. To audiences in Philadelphia, New Haven, Washington, Baltimore, and Buffalo he preached his simple lesson of kindness to animals.

His own work in New York City was helped by an unusual circumstance. A dying man asked to see Henry Bergh. Bergh went to visit the man at a city hospital and listened to his story. His name was Henry Bonard, and he had made a fortune trapping animals for their pelts. In recompense for his slaughter, he left the ASPCA over $100,000 in his will. With the money, the society purchased a new headquarters building at Fourth Avenue and Twenty-second Street, established an animal shelter, and also erected a drinking fountain for city horses.

One day, as Henry Bergh was walking to the new headquarters, he heard mewing as he passed a structure being built nearby. He went over to the workmen, and they told him that a cat had been foolish enough to stray into one of the hollow walls of the building. The animal had been crying for days, but work had to continue. "That cat must be rescued," Henry ordered, "even if the wall has to come down."

He waited for four hours while grumbling workmen, under threat of arrest, removed the wall block by block. A crowd gathered to watch. At last, out crawled an emaciated cat. Scooping it up into his arms, Henry Bergh carried it to the ASPCA shelter. Such situations

The ASPCA headquarters at Twenty-Second Street.

showed New Yorkers and the country that the ASPCA meant business. They had the law on their side and they meant to use it.

In his lectures, Henry liked to astonish his audiences with statistics. "Animals contribute in a thousand ways to our comforts and necessities," he told them. "Over eighty-five million animals labored for the daily need of Americans. Cows contributed over six million pounds of butter, five million pounds of cheese, thirty-six million gallons of milk. Sheep gave ninety million pounds of wool. The busy little bee gave fifteen million pounds of honey. Imagine the consequences if we were deprived of animals. Could we get along without them? We could not! And still some claim that they deserve no sympathy."

"It seems but yesterday," a New York editor wrote, "that at every step of his crusade against cruelty, Henry Bergh was met with official hindrances, with sneers and ridicule from the press. All manner of impediments blocked his mission. It hardly seems possible that one quiet gentleman could work such a revolution in so brief a time."

Henry Ward Beecher, a city minister, paid this tribute to Henry Bergh. Beecher said that when Bergh entered Heaven,

Will there not be a commotion among animals. The birds will tell it. The beasts of the field will know it. Even tropical turtles will shed tears. Elephants will bear him up; the spirit of released horses will prance; cats will

purr with celestial satisfaction, and rub his legs with beseeching caresses. Dogs, without number, will turn their lustrous eyes upon him with gratitude. Yes, the whole air will be full of emancipated animals, all eager to greet and honor their benefactor.

· 1874 ·
Save the Children

There were some harsh critics who accused Henry Bergh of favoring animals over humans. They claimed that he would rather aid animals than aid his fellowman. "The children of New York are sadly in want of a champion," wrote one, "and children are more precious than dogs or horses."

Henry Bergh was not blind to the condition of some children in the city. In making his rounds, he saw the poverty and neglect. Infants were abandoned, and homeless children wandered the streets. They begged for food or pennies. They dropped to sleep in hallways and cellars and city parks. Their situation was a scandal, and no one seemed to care. There were a few overworked orphanages, and some organizations distributed food and clothing, but most people tried to ignore the problem of New

Homeless orphans gather at a steam grate to keep warm.

York's "half-starved and dirty little wretches."

Although Henry Bergh had sympathy for the children, he felt that his work was to speak for animals, not children. However, in 1874, a case of child abuse captured his attention. A church worker, Mrs. Etta Wheeler, heard of the cruel treatment of a child named Mary Ellen. She was living with a Mrs. Connolly and worked for her as a servant. The child was beaten daily with a whip, and her screams were heard by neighbors. Everyone knew that Mary Ellen was in danger. Mrs. Wheeler tried to rescue the girl but could get help from no one. Neither the police nor charitable organizations wanted to get involved. In desperation, she approached Henry Bergh. After all, she reasoned, Mary Ellen was the same as an abused animal.

Henry Bergh was moved by her story, and within hours he and several ASPCA officers invaded the Connolly apartment and rescued Mary Ellen. The nine-year-old was filthy and in rags. She had bruises and welts all over her body. One cheek was slashed and bleeding.

Forty-eight hours after Mrs. Wheeler talked with Henry Bergh, Mary Ellen's case was before the court. A spectator in court that day reported:

I was in the courtroom full of men with stern looks. I saw a child brought in, carried in a horse blanket. The sight of her made the men weep. I saw her laid at the feet of the judge, who turned his face away. I heard the voice of Henry Bergh, "The child is an animal," he said. "If there is no justice for it as a human being, it shall at least have the rights of the dog in the street. It shall not be abused!" And, as I looked I knew I was where the first chapter of children's rights was written. For from that dingy courtroom came forth the New York Society for the Prevention of Cruelty to Children with all it has meant to the world's life. It is spreading in lands and among people who never spoke the name of New York or Mary Ellen.

Mary Ellen was given to kind foster parents, and Mrs. Connolly was sentenced to a year in prison for her cruelty.

"Could there not be a society for children?" Mrs. Wheeler asked Henry. He took her hand and promised, "There will be one!"

In a short time, Henry Bergh composed the society's purpose.

The undersigned, desirous of rescuing the unprotected children of this city and State from the cruelty and demoralization which neglect and abandonment engender, hereby engage to aid, with their sympathy and support the organization and working of a Children's Protection Society.

It was signed by Henry Bergh, by the lawyer for the ASPCA, Elbridge Gerry, and by John Wright, a wealthy Quaker who became the first president of the Society for the Prevention of Cruelty to Children (SPCC). The society was incorporated by the state of New York, and Cornelius Vanderbilt, the millionaire, promised to give "all the money you want."

The society shared office space with the ASPCA, and Henry Bergh was its vice president. There it had a lot to do in New York.

In those days, discipline was harsh. Children were beaten and burned by abusive parents. Drunken fathers used horsewhips on their children or clubbed them with baseball bats. It was not unusual to find children with broken noses or torn ears. In its first year, the SPCC investigated over three hundred cases of child abuse.

Before the enactment of child labor laws in

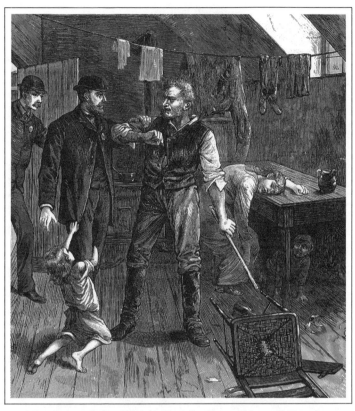

Members of the Society for the Prevention of Cruelty
to Children protect an abused child.

the twentieth century prohibiting the employment of children for hard labor, children had little protection. Like dogs, poor children were used to walk treadmills. They slaved from dawn to dusk in factories and mines. They worked as house servants and were indentured to tradesmen. The abuse of children was rampant. They were taken by criminals and taught to steal and pick pockets. And they were used for prostitution. The Society for the Prevention of Cruelty to Children had much to accomplish. Not only did the SPCC have to rescue children from abuse, but it also had to work to have protective legislation enacted.

The idea of the SPCC spread just as rapidly as had that of the SPCA. In a short time, other states formed societies modeled after the original SPCC. Often these societies joined hands

Children were often beaten
and forced to beg on the streets for their masters.

with the local SPCA groups to preserve the link between the two. But Henry Bergh wanted to keep the two groups separate in New York.

"You cannot serve two masters," he told a friend. "Either one or the other will suffer—or both!" He always insisted that each group do its own work. And although he remained a member of the executive committee of the SPCC, he remained loyal to his first purpose—the rights of God's dumb creatures.

·1878·
The Sportsmen

Henry Bergh once said, "To me there is always something indescribably sad in the word 'kill.' Let us kill an animal, but let it be done with sorrow and pity; if we are not ashamed to kill blamelessly, let us at least sin with discretion— let us eat flesh but let it be for hunger and not for wantonness."

Many of Henry Bergh's friends and New York neighbors killed for sport. Many of these people donated money to the ASPCA and applauded its work; yet they did not consider their animal sports cruel. To them, there was a distinction. But to Henry Bergh, it was another unjust cruelty, and he fought against it.

Pigeon shooting became a favorite sport of marksmen after the Civil War. Birds were released and shot at. Many were killed and many were wounded. Legs were shot off, wings shattered, and bills broken. Birds had pins stuck under their wings to make them more "lively." Pepper, tobacco, or turpentine was rubbed into the birds' eyes. This made them whirl about and added more "fun" to the shoot. At one Brooklyn shoot, over sixteen thousand pigeons were killed or wounded. One spectator described the scene as "an acre of blood and feathers."

Another popular "sport" was the hounding of deer. In the American version of this ancient English sport of stag hunting, a circle of dogs cornered a deer, driving it toward the water. When it took refuge in the lake, it was killed. Hotels in the mountains offered special deer-hounding weekends. "Dog hunting and water butchery are not sport," Henry Bergh protested. "It is simply murder!"

Pig sticking was another pastime. This was popular in rural America. Pigs were chased and jabbed with sharp sticks and spikes. When they were sufficiently wounded, they bled to death. Geese were also victims of this same "sport."

But the most fashionable animal sport was fox hunting. There were many hunting clubs, and the wealthy delighted in it. It was an activity surrounded by ritual, with special hunting costumes and hunt suppers and hunt breakfasts.

In a fox hunt, a live fox is chased by hunters mounted on horses and by a pack of hunting dogs. The chase goes on until the fox is cornered and killed. Often it is torn apart by the angry dogs.

It was not easy to attack these sports. Often Henry Bergh had to attack his friends and supporters. Yet he was the avowed enemy of cruelty where he found it. He did not care what it was called.

"Pigeon shooting prepares sportsmen to defend the country in case of war," reasoned one sportsman.

"Then why not man hunting instead," Bergh responded. "This would better preparation!"

"The fox kills hens. We are doing a service for the farmers," a hunter argued.

Henry replied by reciting an old verse:

A fox is killed by twenty men
That fox, you see, just killed a hen
A gallant act no doubt is here,
All wicked foxes ought to fear,
When twenty dogs and twenty men
Can kill a fox that killed a hen.

· 1880 ·

P. T. Barnum

Not far from Henry and Matilda Bergh's home on Fifth Avenue lived Phineas T. Barnum.

It was Barnum who boasted, "There is a fool born every minute." Barnum had spent his life entertaining and fooling the public. He was a born showman and charged people to view various freaks and feats. His Broadway Museum and Menagerie was the hit of New York City. Here one could watch the "daring young man on the flying trapeze" or stare in wonder at wild animals and circus freaks.

One afternoon, Henry Bergh joined the young of all ages visiting the Broadway Museum. Bergh, who made his reputation by protecting animals, visited Barnum, who made his reputation by exploiting animals. This dangerous mix was bound to explode.

At first view, Henry Bergh was satisfied that

Barnum's animals seemed well fed and housed. But then he spied a keeper placing a live rabbit in the cage of a boa constrictor. He was outraged and questioned the keeper. "It won't eat a dead animal," the man explained. "It will only devour a live one. It's nature's way!" The explanation did not satisfy Henry Bergh. He charged Barnum with being a "barbarian," making money from "amusement which consists in the prolonged torture of an innocent creature."

Barnum responded to the charge by appealing to a Harvard scientist, Louis Agassiz. Agassiz testified that "there is no other way to induce snakes to eat their food other than in the natural manner—that is alive."

That was the end of the first confrontation between Bergh and Barnum. Others erupted over the years.

Barnum's museum suffered several bad fires. One in 1868 destroyed a number of animals. Another in 1872 brought down the museum building and burned or suffocated most of Barnum's menagerie. Henry Bergh and the ASPCA investigated and accused Barnum of "incarcerating poor helpless dumb beasts in iron cages within the tinder-like walls" of an inadequate building. The charge was not unjustified.

The fire at Barnum's new Hippodrome in November 1872

Many of the animals were trapped and could not escape the flames. But Barnum managed to escape prosecution. He went on to build Madison Square Garden to house a new circus and zoo. He called it "The Greatest Show on Earth."

In April of 1880, another head-on collision occurred between the two men. Barnum exhibited a horse named Salamander. It was trained to run through a flaming doorway and then to jump through flaming hoops. At the first performance, Salamander singed his tail and mane. When Henry Bergh learned of this, he complained about the stunt, calling it "an act of cruelty and terror."

Barnum replied that the act had been carried out in a European circus for years without any problems. The singed hair was a minor concern. Since the circus was attracting over five thousand people each day, he had no intention of eliminating the act. Salamander, the Fire Horse, was the main attraction.

City officials joined the controversy. They expressed concern over the safety of the building. The fire department stationed men at every performance. Henry Bergh, however, was not about to wait for city action. Using the powers given to him by law, he ordered Barnum to discontinue the act. In Bergh's view, the act was cruelty to an animal. For a while, Barnum obeyed the order. Then, on April 19, 1880, he announced that Salamander, the Fire Horse, would return as the featured performance. The announcement electrified the city. Everyone expected a confrontation.

On the appointed day, Barnum entered the ring and startled the audience by announcing that he himself would go through the flaming hoops and prove that they were harmless. He then walked through the flaming rings. The audience cheered wildly. Then Salamander, the Fire Horse, bounded onto the stage and followed Barnum through the hoops. The *New York Evening Post* reported that "Mr. Barnum has got the better of Mr. Bergh this time!"

As it turned out, the "fire" was a special chemical fire that created little heat. Moreover, the horse's hide was protected with a solution of alum water. This offered double protection. The entire act was "show business."

Over the years, the two men learned to respect each other. Henry Bergh came to recognize Barnum's knowledge of animals. And Barnum admired Henry Bergh's zeal. He pointed out, "Mr. Bergh and I work together in protecting dumb brutes." In return, the ASPCA president called Barnum "one of the most humane and kind-hearted men living."

Later on, in a letter to Henry Bergh, Barnum wrote:

No one has a greater respect for your character, your good intentions and the cause you represent than myself. Your name and memory will rightfully be honored and revered through coming ages. But, my dear sir, you are human and sometimes err. In your zeal for dumb animals, you occasionally ignore or despise the feelings and just interests of your fellow men. You sometimes abuse the power placed in your hands, by perhaps un-wittingly using it as a despot, and thereby injuring the good cause you desire to benefit.

· 1883 ·
The Great Meddler

In 1883, a newspaper referred to Henry Bergh as "the Great Meddler." Not only did he champion animal rights, but he went on to champion other causes as well. He surprised many people when he advocated the old-fashioned whipping post for minor offenders. What manner of man is this? some asked. He complains about an overworked horse yet wants to whip his fellowman. He also advocated capital punishment. For these stands, he was severely rebuked in the newspapers. Why, they asked, did Bergh favor animals over men? "God gave the animal feeling and man reason," he answered. "If a man abuses his powers, he should be made to suffer. Men with brutal passions and blunted intellects can only be taught humanity by fear."

In 1881, Bergh persuaded a lawmaker to introduce legislation in New York that would have wife beaters flogged. Before the age of women's rights, many wives who were mistreated by ignorant husbands had no way to get justice. Henry Bergh stepped forward as the champion of the "weaker sex." He demanded that husbands who abused their wives get a dose of their own medicine. Again he was attacked by the press. "Some idiots think it is wrong to whip a wretch who beats a women," he answered. "But how else shall we answer the cries of the mothers, sisters, and wives of our land?"

His position prompted one politician to remark, "Mr. Bergh will be bringing us back to the Middle Ages, with thumb screws and the Inquisition. I can never sanction that!"

The notion of whipping wife beaters became a favorite crusade of the Great Meddler. He frequently introduced the subject in his lectures along with his pleas for animals.

A cartoonist in *Puck* magazine pictured Henry Bergh's "Dual Nature." At one time and the same time, he is looking at horses and dogs, and he hands a whip to a wife to use on her offending husband.

Another of Henry Bergh's causes was the hope that eventually people would become

Puck's caricature of "Mr. Bergh's Dual Nature"

vegetarians. He was fond of preaching that the abolition of meat eating would result in the physical and moral improvement of the human race. Here again he stepped on dangerous territory. He was not a vegetarian himself. He claimed that he ate meat "out of habit" and added that "the least appearance of blood, because of insufficient cooking, shocks my sensibilities."

Neither did wearing a fur-lined coat in the winter seem to bother him. He could not see the incongruity of enforcing the anticruelty laws on New York streets while wearing fur-lined coat and fur boots. When his meat eating and fur wearing were pointed out to him, he said that animals may be used, but they must be killed painlessly. So while urging others to give up meat, he continued to enjoy his chicken and beef dinners. He continued to wear his fur-lined coat and even bought Mrs. Bergh an ermine cape and muff. He left to his descendants in the animal rights movement the protest against the wearing of furs.

Newspaper cartoons often depicted Bergh with a long nose. The depiction meant that he stuck his nose into and meddled in others' business. Yet many times his crusade against cruelty to animals demanded that he meddle. He had no choice during those ruthless years of the late nineteenth century.

Up until then, very few people thought that animals had rights. As one Pennsylvania preacher had put it, "The Good Book says that man shall have dominion over beasts. They're ours to use as we please."

This same thinking continued on into the mid–twentieth century in a statement made by Pope Pius XII. It said that when animals are butchered or killed, "their cries should not arouse unreasonable compassion any more than do red-hot metals undergoing the blows of the hammer, or branches crackling when they are pruned, or wheat being ground by the milling machine."

It was small comfort to Henry Bergh to know that the Royal SPCA in England had been successfully operating for forty years before his American crusade began. He had to break new ground in his native land and attempt to change entrenched attitudes. It was not easy to take on the truckmen and butchers and politicians. He fought ignorance and barbarity. Considering his background, his success was remarkable. He took the ridicule and criticism hurled at him with dignity. He was always a gentlemen. He despised all cruelty. With compassion, he reached out to include the abused children in his crusade for justice. He reached out to protect the battered wife. Though he may have overstepped his ground at times, the Great Meddler always had justice in mind.

While philosophers and theologians grappled with the "animal problem," as they called the moral aspect of cruelty to animals, Henry Bergh did what he had to do.

Over the years, he championed one cause after another—everything from fire prevention to the temperance movement. With persistence and a belief in his convictions, he went his meddling way!

"I am not a lawyer," he explained, "but I have that which is the foundation of that profession—zeal and common sense, and I lose very few cases . . . in pleading for the punishment of brute torturers, slaughterhouses, and everywhere else where cruelty lurks. I visit, and I neither fear disease nor ridicule! One thing seems to be generally admitted by press and public; that is the Society is fast becoming a power for doing good and terrifying workers of cruelty. I regard a helpless child in the same light as a dumb animal. Both are God's creatures; my duty is to aid them."

· 1885 ·
Other Voices: Other Views

From time to time, Henry Bergh had threats made against his life. Often large and inky drawings of the skull and crossbones would cross his desk. Once this ominous note reached him:

I desire to warn you that a conspiracy is afoot against your life. The date has been set for your death. It will be Thursday evening at nine.

The note was signed, "A Friend."

"I don't frighten easily," he would say, and usually tossed the warnings into the wastebasket.

One time a cruel wagon driver lunged at him with an iron rod. It just grazed his scalp. Fish heads and the bloody entrails of dead animals were thrown to him. More than once when Mrs. Bergh greeted him at home after a day on the job, his clothing was stained with animal blood. Despite it all, he took it in good humor and went about his work.

A group that constantly harassed Henry Bergh were those doctors and scientists who practiced vivisection. Vivisection is an operation performed on a living animal. In the beginning, these experiments were conducted without the use of anesthesia. "Of all the horrible pains inflicted on animals," Bergh said, "those done in the name of science are the most fearful."

Vivisection had its opponents when it was first introduced in England. Henry Bergh declared war on vivisection in America. He vigorously opposed the cutting, burning, and maiming of live animals in the name of science. He charged hospitals and doctors doing it with cruelty to animals. Their answer was, "The ultimate object is the relief of human suffering and the cure of human disease." Moreover, they pointed out, scientific experiments were excluded from the anticruelty laws.

In response, Henry Bergh tried to change the law. Year after year, he presented an antivivisection bill to the New York legislature. Year after year, his efforts were opposed by medical science. Whenever he lectured against vivisection, doctors and medical students packed the halls to boo and hiss. The morality of vivisection has not yet been determined, and those who follow in Henry Bergh's footsteps still fight against it.

While all this was going on, other people paid tribute to Henry Bergh. He was nominated by a city newspaper as New York's First Citizen. A newspaper editorial proclaimed, "Bergh for Mayor." Two decades of crusading for the rights of animals had finally brought to him the recognition he justly deserved.

"Mr. Bergh should be encouraged and cheered," a magazine article urged. And after years of laughter and insults, many agreed. Henry himself never doubted his mission. "I stand between right and wrong; between mercy and cruelty," he said. No reward or praise pleased him more than imitation. He was proudest of the spread of his crusade.

Some compared Bergh to the Great Buddha in his teaching of kindness to animals. Others likened him to Saint Francis of Assisi. He dismissed such lofty praise. Yet, his life was directed by a verse he often quoted. It is from "The Rime of the Ancient Mariner" by Samuel Taylor Coleridge:

He prayeth well, who loveth well
Both man and bird and beast
He prayeth best, who loveth best
All things both great and small
For the dear God who loveth us
He made and loveth all.

"As I understand the justice and wisdom of Almighty God," he told a clergyman, "He entertains no partiality for any of His creatures, but His affection is extended to all alike. The insect in the plant, the moth hovering about the candle's flame, even the life which inhabits a drop of water, is as much an object of His Providence as the mightiest monarch on his throne."

In the years of his leadership of the ASPCA, over fourteen thousand cases of cruelty to animals were prosecuted. Over thirty-five thousand disabled animals were rescued. More than twenty-five thousand disabled horses were humanely destroyed. Forty-four SPCAs served North and South America. Other animal groups formed, and humane associations combined the rescue of animals and children.

"Those who imagined that this Society was going to be a nine days' wonder," Bergh boasted, "now know it is here to stay."

· 1888 ·
The Great Blizzard

As the years went by, the toils and troubles of old age visited the president of the ASPCA.

Henry Bergh was quite vain about revealing his true age. In 1886, during his seventy-third year, he boasted, "I'm never going to be more than forty-five!" Yet, protest as he might, old age was upon him. His colds were becoming more frequent, and upset stomachs plagued him. In 1883, he had fallen on the street in New York and broken his collarbone.

More disturbing to Henry was the illness of his wife, Matilda. The couple had enjoyed many happy years of married life. However, in the 1870s, Matilda developed a spinal problem and had to be placed in a nursing home in upstate New York. She lingered on there, but eventually her sickness affected her mind. At the end, when Henry visited her, she failed to recognize him.

Henry stayed at his home on Fifth Avenue and carried on. Often he was joined by his nephews, Henry and Edwin. He was training them to carry on his work in the ASPCA. The demands of his mission still used up most of his waking hours, but he realized that his career was drawing to a close.

Aside from animals, his only other interests were the theater and collecting art, both of which he had pursued since his youth. He crowded paintings and sculpture into his Fifth Avenue house, and he seldom missed an opening night at the theater. He had many friends among actors and actresses. Of course, many of them made large donations to his society.

Then, on the night of March 11, 1888, snow swirled through the streets of New York. Strong winds tore roofs off houses, and, by midnight, there was enough snow to prevent any travel in the city. The storm continued and even increased in intensity. The famous Blizzard of '88 was wreaking havoc on the eastern seaboard.

Sheltered from the storm in the bedroom of

A scene of the blizzard of 1888

his home, Henry Bergh lay in bed close to death. Chronic bronchitis, coupled with a serious heart condition, had weakened him. Too many days and nights on the city streets searching out animal abuse had finally taken their toll. Now Bergh struggled to draw each breath. His doctor was called, but he was delayed by the storm. The snow, as one observer put it, was "up to my armpits!"

Early on the morning of March 12, 1888, the doctor arrived. But he was too late. Henry Bergh had died a few hours earlier.

The city slowly dug its way out of the great

storm. By noon, a few carriages were able to move through the streets. Despite the conditions, Bergh's body was taken to Saint Mark's Church. This was where, nearly fifty years before, young Henry and Matilda had spoiled the elaborate wedding planned for them. Officers of the ASPCA carried the flower-covered casket. At the funeral were numerous politicians and city officials. The entire staffs of the animals' and children's societies were there. And there were hundreds of floral tributes. One of them was a big wreath of white roses framing a photograph of a family pet. The card was inscribed "To Henry Bergh, Samson's Best Friend." During the ceremonies, a young girl entered the church with her dog. They walked up the aisle, and she prayed before the casket.

At last, Henry Bergh's body was laid on a wagon pulled by a team of horses and taken to the cemetery for burial. Among the floral pieces was a large basket of flowers from P. T. Barnum, and it was Barnum who paid this final tribute:

Mr. Bergh was a kind and noble-hearted man. We should remember that no man is perfect, and that, with all his faults and shortcomings, Henry Bergh, president of the Society for the Prevention of Cruelty to Animals, is to be honored and respected for his unselfish devotion to such an excellent cause.

Henry Bergh was gone, but his mission grew and multiplied. By the beginning of the twentieth century, there were 659 societies in the United States for the prevention of cruelty, handling over two million cases of animal abuse annually. And the concept of prevention of cruelty gave rise to concern for animal welfare education. Instances of cruelty declined as peo-

Henry Bergh stops an overloaded wagon and warns the driver.

ple became more aware of the problem and programs were presented in schools. By 1925, an SPCA officer could report, "In former days, an agent would make two or three arrests a day. Now an agent may walk the streets all day without seeing a case demanding interference."

Henry Bergh's spirit lives on in the hearts and minds of his fellow Americans and people everywhere who have concern for animals. His battle to correct the cruel habits of a nation makes him unique in the history of social change.

Today's
Henry Berghs

Although most people speak of the SPCA as though it were a national organization, there are in fact many SPCA's. Because of the country's size and various state laws, each SPCA is independent. They may be loosely federated, but they function independently. In addition there are many other animal groups. There are humane societies; anticruelty societies; animal welfare societies and animal rescue leagues. There are over one thousand animal protection organizations in the United States alone and membership runs into the millions. Henry Bergh's crusade for animals has passed on to others. Animals are not without their friends.

The animal abuse opposed by Henry Bergh is rare today. The horse is no longer the prime means of transportation. Slaughterhouses and meat packers are carefully regulated. Blood sports have declined in popularity. The country at large has a new standard of feeling and awareness about the treatment of animals. And Henry Bergh helped to create it.

Today there are other concerns. There is growing opposition to cruel and unusual animal experimentation. Some animal rights groups have raided laboratories to rescue animals. They have exposed the horrors of some animal experiments.

There are organized efforts to prevent the clubbing of baby seals along Canada's eastern coast and the slaughter of African elephants for their ivory tusks. There are some who oppose hunting and the wearing of fur coats. There are even those who oppose the eating of meat.

Cruelty to animals has not been abolished. There are still places in the United States where cock fights are legal. There are states with weak or ineffective animal legislation. Cruelty and abuse are still with us. The work begun in the United States by Henry Bergh is far from finished. In the animal kingdom, we alone possess the use of language and reason. We can recognize the difference between what is harmful and what is not. If we do not fully understand our relationship with animals, we must keep on trying. By learning more about them and by listening to those who speak for them we may reach some understanding.

Animals are not our underlings. They are fellow creatures. Saint Francis of Assisi called them "brothers and sisters." The Bible speaks of a "peaceable kingdom" where all creatures live together in harmony. Someday we may reach that peaceable kingdom and come to a full understanding of our relationship with other living things. Until then, the wisdom of Henry Bergh reminds us that "men will be just to men when they are kind to animals."

Henry Bergh's SPCA, founded "to provide effective means for the prevention of cruelty to animals throughout the United States," is the original and national organization. It alone has the right to call itself the ASPCA—the American Society for the Prevention of Cruelty to Animals. It has members in every state who support its multimillion-dollar operation. Although its focus is the care and protection of New York City's animals, its educational and legislative efforts are nationwide in their scope and influence. The ASPCA leads the way in carrying on Henry Bergh's crusade for kindness.

Bibliography

Carson, Gerald. *Men, Beasts and Gods.* New York, 1972.

Coleman, Sydney H. *Humane Society Leaders in America.* New York, 1924.

Floyd-Jones, Thomas. *Backward Glances.* New York, 1941.

Kaufman, Martin, and Herbert Kaufman. "Salamander the Fire Horse." *American History Illustrated.* October 1980.

Lynch, Denis T. *The Wild Seventies.* New York, 1941.

McCrea, R. C. *The Humane Movement.* New York, 1910.

Peattie, Donald C. "He Invented a New Kind of Goodness." *Reader's Digest.* October 1941.

Rowley, Francis H. *The Humane Idea.* Boston, 1912.

Smith, Stephen. *The City That Was.* New York, 1911.

Steele, Sulma. *Angel in Top Hat.* New York, 1942.

Webb, Alexander S. "America's First Humanitarian." *National Humane Review.* April 1941.

Werner, M. R. *Barnum.* New York, 1923.

Westermarck, Edward. *Christianity and Morals* (Chapter XIX). London, 1939.

Wilson, James Grant. *The History of the City of New York.* New York, 1939.

Index